Ciao! How are you world?

WRITTEN BY ANNA MACCARONIO

Questo libro e' dedicato
a tutti i genitori del mondo.

This book is dedicated
to all the parents of the world.

Themis Books

Good Counsel

2021

A children's book written with the mindfulness of your child's emotional intelligence as priority, while exposing them to the Italian language and a world of cultural diversity.

Un libro scritto per dare priorità
all'intelligenza e alla salute emotiva di tuo
figlio, esponendolo, nel contempo,
sia alla lingua italiana che a
un mondo multiculturale.

Where do emotions come from?

Our emotions develop in our **brains**,
which are inside our heads and
shaped like the inside of open *walnuts*.

WHAT ARE EMOTIONS?

**Emotions are feelings that
dictate how we react in a specific moment.**

All the emotions we feel are **right**. The most important
thing is to find a way to **name them**! Only then can
we choose to make mindful decisions based
on our self-reflection.

Da dove provengono le **emozioni** (eh-MOTE-zee-o-nay)?

Le nostre emozioni si sviluppano nel **cervello** (cher-VELL-o), che si trova nella nostra testa e ha la forma dell'interno di una **noce** (NO-chay).

COSA SONO LE EMOZIONI?

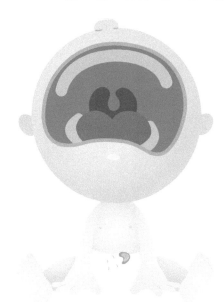

Le emozioni sono dei sentimenti che dettano cosa proviamo in un particolare momento.

Tutte le emozioni che proviamo sono **giuste** (gee-OO-stay), l'importante è chiamarle con il loro **nome (NO-mee).** Solo così possiamo fare scelte consapevoli basate sulla nostra auto-riflessione.

Let's name our emotions together:

Nominiamo insieme
le nostre emozioni :

HAPPINESS

Gaia is super **happy** to spend the day outside, eating her gelato!

FELICITÁ
(fay-LEE-chee-tah)

Gaia è molto **felice (FAY-lee-chay)** di stare fuori all'aria aperta a mangiare il suo gelato!

SADNESS

Damiano is **sad** to go to his first day of school and leave his mom.

TRISTEZZA
(TREE-stays-zah)

Damiano è **triste (TREE-stay)** di dover affrontare la sua prima giornata di scuola e lasciare la sua mamma.

ANGER

Davide and Beatrice broke Rossana's doll, and they are now **angry** because their mom is upset at them!

RABBIA
(er-RAH-bee-ah)

_____

Davide e Beatrice hanno rotto la bambola di Rossana, e sono arrabbiati (ah-RAH-bee-ah-tee) perché la mamma li ha rimproverati!

CALM

The mothers and their kids are happy to spend a day of **calm** on the countryside.

SERENITÁ
(SEH-reh-neet-tah)

Le mamme e i loro figli sono contenti di trascorrere una giornata in **serenitá (SEH-reh-neet-tah)** in campagna.

FEAR

Alice is scared of the dark.

PAURA
(pah-UR-rah)

Alice ha
paura (pah-UR-rah)
del buio.

LOVE

Love for our four
legged friends.

AMORE
(ah-MO-ray)

L'amore (ah-MO-ray)
per i nostri amici
a quattro zampe.

SELF LOVE

L'AMORE PER SE STESSI

(lamore per se stessi)

ABOUT THE AUTHOR

I grew up in Misterbianco, a small town in Sicily (province of Catania). I was an only child and I always dreamed as a little girl to have a big family of siblings of **every race in the world.**

This conviction of mine reflects and takes life in this very book!

———— • ————

My childhood was very happy; my parents exposed me to many different sports, hobbies, and a variety of friends growing up...until I turned seven. That year my parents separated and my dad moved all the way to a different country (Malta). Soon after, my parents divorced, which, at the time, was not customary in an old country like Italy. As a child of divorced parents, I grew resentful and suffered tremendously because I did not know how to cope with my emotions in a healthy way. I always felt I was the odd one out in class who had to choose between mom or dad. By the time I reached adolescence, my anger and frustration resulted in a rebellion which took years to overcome. Of course, divorce isn't the only source of emotional trauma children may face throughout their childhoods. Death, illness and loss are all part of the human experience. Regardless of the source of trauma, parents need to make sure that children understand their own feelings.

Kids **throw tantrums** towards parents because they are trying to communicate emotions.

I now know how important it is to get a hold of my emotions, to recognize what they are, when they are coming up, and address them accordingly. **Emotions play a major role** on how we experience life as adults. The key is to be **aware** of all the emotions that go on in our head. Our brains are beautiful and **delightfully complicated.**

This awarenesss helps us to be responsible adults, respect other people, and respect the diversity of this world.

Understanding that **we learn our emotions from our parents,** as they impart the good and the bad stuff in us is crucial in **educating kids.** I strongly believe that kids are our most valuable worldly investment, and because they carry the **wealth of humanity for generations to come**, it is important that we impart healthy behavioral and cognitive habits in them. It starts by teaching them how to **name their emotions.**

———— • ————

When we are kids we are sponges and our personalities are shaped by the ages of 5 or 6. My father was gone a lot for work while I was growing up which forced my mom and me to be on our own.

———— • ————

As a teenager I expressed a lot of rebellion, towards my parents. So much so that I decided to get married at 18 and move to the U.S.A. with my then husband. Throughout the years I had trouble letting go of my pain, my past wounds (which showed up in my love relationships as well as friendships) and resentment towards my dad and the people who hurt me. The last 15 years have been an intricate journey in my life.

Honing in the discovery of one's purpose, is crucial to help build a sense of self and form authentic relationships, both love and friendship related.

———— • ————

The **3 key factors** in any relationship are **communication, respect** and **trust.** The way we communicate, respect and trust other people around us everyday, is how we treat our significant others, and become responsible parents. I am still learning how to refine these skills. And **it is ok to not always be ok!**

———— • ————

I have great admiration and particular love for kids; in fact, the many kids I have encountered all over the world inspired me to write this book. Kids are our future—let's teach them how to be mindful of others and themselves. Our role in the world is exponential from the inside of us to the outside of us.

———— • ————

Inside of each adult, is a little boy or little girl; our spirit of pure joy and adventure is the driver that makes us who we authentically are. This book is my way of giving back to the world by sharing my knowledge of Italian, together with a glimpse of various cultures with all of you!

With all my love and respect for you parents of the world.

Anna

PRONOUNCIATION GUIDE

in order of appearance

emozioni (eh-MOTE-zee-o-nay): Emotions

cervello (cher-VELL-o): Brain

noce (NO-chay): Walnut

giuste (gee-OO-stay): Right

nome (NO-mee): Name

felicitá (fay-LEE-chee-tah): Happiness

felice (FAY-lee-chay): Happy

tristezza (TREE-stays-zah): Sadness

triste (TREE-stay): Sad

rabbia (er-RAH-bee-ah): Anger

arrabbiato (ah-RAH-bee-ah-toe): Angry (boy)

arrabbiata (ah-RAH-bee-ah-tah): Angry (girl)

serenitá (SEH-reh-neet-tah): Calm

paura (pah-UR-rah): Fear

amore (ah-MO-ray): Love

l'amore per se stessi (lamore per se stessi): Self love

Thank you for reading me,
bye bye!

Grazie per avermi letto,
ciao ciao!

My home city Catania, with the Etna volcano erupting in Sicily

This book's purpose is to bring emotional
awareness to parents and their babies.

If we start implementing healthy behaviors
and come up with solutions before the
issues arise we may be of help
not only to our own families,
but to the world in general.

CPSIA information can be obtained
at www.ICGtesting.com
Printed in the USA
LVHW072301181121
703815LV00004B/52